THE MARABOU WHO CROSSED THE SEA

The Marabou Who Crossed the Sea
Copyright © 2026 ROHANNA SSANYU
All rights reserved. No part of this publication may be reproduced or transmitted in any form or by any means without the prior written permission of the publisher, except for brief excerpts for the purpose of criticism and review.

For permissions and information on ordering books, contact operations@smallharborpublishing.com.

Cover art: Rohanna Ssanyu, "Black Feathers, Pink Flesh"
Cover design: Jessy Montoya
Editor: Jessie Truong
Publisher: Allison Blevins
Executive Editor: Kristiane Weeks-Rogers
Managing Editor: Bianca Dagostino

THE MARABOU WHO CROSSED THE SEA
ROHANNA SSANYU
ISBN 978-1-957248-63-9
Harbor Editions,
an imprint of Small Harbor Publishing
Special thanks to: The Wild & Precious Life Series and Kristin Vandeventer

The Marabou Who Crossed the Sea

Rohanna Ssanyu

Harbor Editions
Small Harbor Publishing

In memory of our jajja,
Catherine Namutebi Nsubuga Kabali,
and the gardens she grew.

(1927-2010)

For Catherine's baby, Rita.

Contents

Fairbanks / 5
Marabou / 6
Papaya Tree / 7
Kampala / 8
I Write to My Mother From a Desk at Kololo School
    with a Borrowed Pen / 10
Uganda Wins Independence in 1962 / 11
Death of the Papaya / 12
Time Traveler Hears Dancing Queen / 14
Uncle Writes / 15
Time Traveler Catches the Akamba Bus / 16
Broken Zipper / 18
Confession / 19
Found in a Connecticut Used Book Store: Africa
    Section (Farthest from the Door) / 20
Notes on Turning Self into Muganda Girl / 21
Grey Crowned Crane / 22
Found in the African Art Collection of a New Haven
    Gallery after the Guard Asks Whether My Son
    Knows the Rules / 23
Kazinga Channel / 25
Found Under a Jar of Buttons / 26
Cousins / 27
Namesake / 28
Boogeyman / 29
African Aviary / 31
Notes of Turning Self into Garden / 32
Have You Become the Dust? / 34
Ink Blot Held to Cloud / 35

Acknowledgments / 36
Glossary / 39

The Marabou Who Crossed the Sea

"I am the sin of memory and the absence of memory."
—Warsan Shire

FAIRBANKS

My eyes opened to the dusk
of midnight
following the day
I understood place,

that I am from
here, and my mother,
someplace else.

In my room
a mosquito buzzed
over a field of pink fireweed
sown in princess carpet,

and in the doorway stood
a grey crowned crane
framed in paper birch
with eyes of water.

It vanished in the blossoms,
reappeared beside my bed.
Mwana wange
genda webake.

I laid a blanket on its back
before I fell asleep again.

MARABOU

The smell of burning plastic, heat,
a city waking heard in horns,
a stork who has moved into town,
an appetite for human trash.

The marabou who crossed the sea!

       A tale for her bazukulu.
       She spreads her arms, her fingers splay.
       Her eyes widen, clouded in time.

Skeletal legs, an inkblot held
to cloud, a grainy beak, pink flesh,
a nape of hair, a head splattered
in orange blood! A sky

and its undertaker, the stork,
follows vultures, snacks on the dead.

       Her voice drops low, the children still.

And when the day will be hot, felt
in warm concrete at dawn, the scent
of gasoline

look up.

PAPAYA TREE

Light hit my mother's eyes
at the same time
a tree snake
slid across her finger,
and as she fell
the ribbon of her green dress,
a gift from London,
reached for the ripe papaya
she had spotted from the ground.
I searched for the tree
that expelled her
at the edge of the family land
now marked
by cement walls,
and I snapped it
with a camera
and placed the photo
next to the twisted face
of a corrupt man, on blue
painted sheetrock
of an American split-level.
As if it were an ancestor,
as if the ancestors
are the things that break us.

KAMPALA

A road sign points to Parliament Av. A pushcart full of jackfruit rolls and the tire of a truck. A dotted dress slips onto a mannequin. It tightens at the hips. A wooden comb picks apart rows. Women cover chests with backpacks, forearms with purse straps. Lips sip tea from plastic cups. Goat meat sizzles in a blackened tray. Fresh braids top heads. A polo shirt reads *Christ Jesus*. Bags of corn pop in the sun. The end of a headscarf flies, water buckets splash. Jeans stack, Hollywood bootlegs pile on plastic sheets. Bristles scrub loafers in a soapy basin. Teeth chew sugarcane.

A baby sleeps against her mother's back in a blanket bluer than scorpion grass. A traffic light turns red. The *New Vision* front cover faces the street. *Pedestrian knocked dead!* Black plastic hits thighs. Hands stack pyramids of passion fruit. The call to prayer echoes down an alleyway white in the midday. A box of cabbage falls from its bed.

Rice piles. A string is cut. A rifle dangles from a hand. Flip flops smack heels. A Bible waves at the intersection. Young hands usher business into shops. Young hands wave customers into taxis. *To Wandegeya, to Nakawa!*

Spit hits the ground. Black boots follow black boots. Bodas jump to hardened dirt. Paws scurry. Cabbage heads roll. Smoke jets from exhaust pipes. A bicycle horn blows.

A driver slams his brakes. Leaves flatten against cement. Yellow jerry cans collapse. A marabou swallows black plastic. An old woman holds a cell phone to her mouth. A councilman looks down from the lamp post. His eyes do not follow the old woman. His eyes follow a young girl in a dotted dress. The machine jams, tangled thread spills.

I WRITE TO MY MOTHER FROM A DESK AT KOLOLO SCHOOL WITH A BORROWED PEN

You stood in relief
to blue snow, to cannoli cake, to hip hop
and low-rise jeans,
to mothers who shopped at Victoria's Secret
and talked to their daughters about sex.

Maama, this place
looks like you when you were young,
when you sang prayers into my ear,
when you wrapped me
in the esuuka you wore to wed.

And the volcanic ash
I flew over to get here, the sea islands lit
in flickering wicks,
the black feathers, the desert gold—
you are as beautiful now.

UGANDA WINS INDEPENDENCE IN 1962

Raindrops fall from plump clouds,
amass in our palms.
Too much,

and it spills between our fingers,
too little and it hangs
like virga and it's gone.

DEATH OF THE PAPAYA

Baby Jonah, who is now three, finds the fallen papaya. It is rotten, but not enough for the marabou to mistake it for a carcass. Baby Jonah loves to play with the slimy seeds—squish them in his palms. Pop them between his toes. He watches the papaya, waiting for signs of life—its patchy yellow, its blackened stem end. Baby Jonah finds his cousins on a mukeka in the garden building a village of sticks. He places the papaya at his feet. Pronounces it dead. Alice scrunches her nose. Rosemary scowls. *Papayas do not drop. They are plucked when ripe.* James smirks. Baby Jonah wails. Knowing too long a cry will alert Jajja, Beatrice, who is now eleven, and the quickest, picks up the fruit. *We will bury it.* Beatrice asks Baby Jonah to give the papaya a name—*Godfrey*, he chooses—and instructs him to grab a handful of fresh jasmine. *Lay it on the skin.* Baby Jonah recites the two children's prayers he knows by heart. Again and again. On the second day, Godfrey attracts flies. Beatrice brings a rolled paper lit from a stove to burn the flowers. Smoke rises, catching the attention of the neighbors past the honeysuckles. They join Baby Jonah in prayer. Beatrice finds a white rag and covers Godfrey. All but its rotten head. *We must dress it properly!* cries James. He has run away from Rosemary and her village. James rips a sheet of bark from a fallen branch and beats it with a rock. A neighbor insists Godfrey be washed and soon returns with a basin and sponge. Beatrice collects water in a jerry can. The children each wash Godfrey of his red mites. Baby Jonah throws handfuls of dirt on Godfrey's skin to hasten the proceedings. James beats the bark smooth. More neighbors arrive. *It is not ready!* scolds Rosemary as she tosses Baby Jonah onto her back. She reveals a pocket of cotton she has pulled and fills the papaya's decay. On the third day, Alice burns her thumb with the jasmine fire. Beatrice soothes it with the sponge. James builds instruments: a rock-and-roll guitar, a drum, a bow harp, a flute, a xylophone made with rocks, cans, and loose strings, boxes and bones. Rosemary and the other elders lay under the tree while Baby Jonah naps on the mukeka, debating which of the surviving papayas will lead the family. Beatrice and James dig the grave. The band plays. Alice leads the children in song. *Weraba, weraba. Otambule mirembe.* The smallest children cry for Godfrey. A boy asks, *will I ripen?* Alice speaks as its mother, the tree, asking for forgiveness. Rosemary and Baby Jonah lower Godfrey. The children scoop their dirt. Jajja appears from behind a rose bush, sucks her teeth, shoos away the neighbors, grabs her white rag, and bats the air. *Put out that fire!*

TIME TRAVELER HEARS DANCING QUEEN

I find my mother in the room she shares
with her sisters listening
to a loud radio. Rain drums
against the roof. She rearranges the items
of her suitcase that will remind her.

I approach. She trusts my eyes,
and lets me hold her youthful hands. I whisper
centuries of stories from the new world
in which she births me—
stories of empires eating,
gobs of lullabies in
mother tongues falling from lips
becoming man-made lakes.

Gwani? she demands and slaps
my hands away. *Gwe olimba!*
You want it for yourself.

UNCLE WRITES

My wife lifted from her body at night,
      petrified our daughters.
She leaped from her window
      and became a swarm of bats.
She left her bones for something else to chew.

TIME TRAVELER CATCHES THE AKAMBA BUS

A bald man in sandals sweats
on the roof loading plastic mesh
bags into the storage bin.

The 1958 engine grumbles. Wives or mothers or
lovers kiss their travelers and hand them
banana pancakes in sweet grass baskets. I see her

standing in a green dress ruffled at the sleeves
pulling on her brother's shirt.
They all hold a piece of him,

a hand,
a shoulder.
I weave through quiet goodbyes to tell them,

this is it. The boy bends to hug
his sister, the bridge of her nose
wrinkles as she smiles,

water swells
in our eyes and I count them—six.
The last time the siblings

are together in life, before the scattering,
before the taped funerals—
the story my mother tells me

in the Subaru, stopped at a crossing,
waiting for the freight train
to pass, twenty-five years later, as I grow

too warm in my Pink Ranger sweater,
driving home from her job
as a nanny for a white family,

the snow, dancing
against the blackness in the headlights—
this is not it.

Memories are deceitful maps.

BROKEN ZIPPER

Upon arriving in America,
the marabou visits a Lord & Taylor at which,
by his luck, he finds a sales clerk from his country.

They greet. He asks for a deeper discount
on a coat from the sales rack.
She laughs, and tells him where in town

to find the closest thing to matoke—
the CTown on North Street.
She is from Kasubi.

He, from Mulago,
but his people, Queen Elizabeth.
They compare relations—

a sister who works at the hospital and takes lunch
under a papaya tree behind the nursing school.
A cousin who frequents the trash piles

along Kawaala Road. He places the coat
made of white feathers, on the counter and winks. *No one
will write me into spring fables with skinny legs alone.*

Mmm, she replies.

CONFESSION

Ancestors,
my cells
forming in the womb
drank the Hi-C
my mother bought
from Safeway.
I was born
a raspberry lime
and wild
berry baby.

FOUND IN A CONNECTICUT USED BOOK STORE: AFRICA SECTION (FARTHEST FROM THE DOOR)
A cut-up spine poem

Don't call me Africa
call me: Mimi, lady, wandering girl,
the eye of the elephant when she was white,

the memory of birds in a season of blood,
the founder, the translator,
a paradise.

Find me unafraid,
between two worlds,
on a camel for the son.

Find me playing the enemy,
on the race to Fashoda,
on a house in the sky.

In the Africa house
do they hear you when you cry
white mischief and the rape of the Nile?

When a crocodile eats the sun
and my traitor's heart,
it's the way things happen.

NOTES ON TURNING SELF INTO MUGANDA GIRL

I crave Luganda
and I stuff myself with words at night
when no one can stop me

Sugary words like
kabalagala that get stuck on my tongue
wash them down with mango seltzer

so when Auntie asks me *do you speak?*
I can burp out a few
or cry them onto my cheeks, or cough them

into her hands
Auntie finds my language
distasteful

so I invite her to sit on my uncovered couch
and serve her lemongrass tea, a decade old
I fall to my knees

and speak nonsense to her
regurgitated words, sticky
Auntie scrunches her nose and tells me

just speak in English
so I curse her in Spanish

GREY CROWNED CRANE

Fastest declining
crane species in the world, Black,
chicks now call themselves.

FOUND IN THE AFRICAN ART COLLECTION OF A NEW HAVEN GALLERY AFTER THE GUARD ASKS WHETHER MY SON KNOWS THE RULES
A cut-up poem made with exhibit labels

A puppet masquerade at the cradle of humankind
made of geometric patterns.

A billion colorful textiles
grouped by vibrant cosmopolitans.
Leopards of leg rattles,
buffalo of calabash gourds and unpredictable actions.
Hyenas adorned in cotton wigs
work out their aggression through dance
and punish those who disturb the community—
the house, the site of power and blood.

The sculptures came into being.

Brass castings, treasures in exile.
Private collections gifted by Mr. and Mrs. Feathers.
Crushed eggshells, horns of secret meaning.
The royal court looks to the future,
to pepper and ivory,
to complex histories on continued display.

The palace is looted!

God of the sea, with aspirations for political office
and future crimes,
sits on a mantle of cotton cloth, singing

while he inserts into his stomach
coins, glass beads, ceremonial swords,
and other antiquities.

KAZINGA CHANNEL

A fish eagle rested
near a spoonbill wading.
On the bank, the buffalo
chewed river grass, the ox birds
dug for juicy ticks,
a hippopotamus
lay atop his brothers.
A grey crowned crane shook
water from its back feathers.
A crocodile drifted
beholding the spoonbill's legs.
It took a bite. The eagle rose,
in sight of fishermen
wading through river grass.
Covered in sand, a baby crocodile
slipped into the shallow.

FOUND UNDER A JAR OF BUTTONS
A cut-up poem made from a letter

Michigan
    7.21.1998

Dearest child.

You will learn I enjoyed the time I spent in Connecticut. Your business? How many bean babies have you bought? Now the point of our being is to know God, to give to all. To worship is to know kindness. PLEASE TRY TO MEMORISE. Thy name is my healing. Ask Mummy to pray. When I go back, you will write to me from memory: books, wishes. Boundless love.

COUSINS

We wear fishnets.
We do not have the medicine to breathe.
We own the land now and we want profit.

We whisper to our lovers on the phone, under the blankets.
We take selfies in fields of red sunflowers.
We question whether fractions can make us whole.

We ask our husbands to call us Yayeri when they think
        about how much they love us.
We become our parents' dreams.
We must now find a way to be free.

We love this woman with thick hair and freckles.
We met her in Haifa, kissed her on the terrace beside the
        cypress tree.
We suck our teeth when we speak English.

We deposit to accounts hidden from the family.
We just say *yes* when our daughter asks if she is aboriginal.
We escape with a man from the islands.

We hum under a turquoise sky as the choir sings.
We are tired of eyes on our bodies.
We know each other through airmail envelopes, stamped in
        the profile of the Queen.

We do not play together as children.
We cannot afford the ticket home to bury Grandmother.
All the men holding her casket are strangers.

NAMESAKE
For Leon

I once watched a lion
in black mane

emerge from a jackalberry
into dawn,

his gaping mouth
and quiet paws,

watch fire eat lines
of lemongrass, controlled by rangers,

and past that, to the border
I was told

was there, to Virunga
and past that, and I looked

with him at a country marked
in red on my paper map.

The lion yawned at blue peaks
and he saw no blood

lines drawn in dirt
as he slid his front legs forward

to stretch, controlled
by his hunger,

this rising sun.

BOOGEYMAN

The colonizers promise his mother he will be good but feed him shillings. He chews with his front teeth. They chip, sharp like a crocodile. You do not meet him before the people serve him poisoned soup. He lives in the shadows of a room—waits in the Turkish tea shop where you write.

You ask your mother if he can swim the ocean. She says he walks on its floor, catches fish in his hair. You stop going to the beach at dusk. Your mother sees him in all the boys, even your own. The man smoking at the bus stop on Dixwell reminds her. She says, *lock your car.* You see him in all the boys, even your own. He is always thirsty. He hits his woman for not being a bottle of gin. He claims her body, expels the others, gnaws at her skin until pink.

A friend invites you to a sleepover. You sit on her butterfly bed and eat the Christmas cookies her father brings you in the blue of the television set. You watch *Don't Look Under the Bed*. Disney monsters have long fingernails. She says the movie has it wrong. *Boogeyman lives in the hallway.* You laugh at her, her cheeks are red. A shadow moves. She does not invite you to sleep over again.

With crayons you draw him in a yellowing wig, a sun hat, a suit jacket pinned in ribbons. You write him a letter and leave it in the corner of a room. You tell him about his daughter, the baby. You love her. Does that mean you love him too? You tell him she wears red lipstick and ties her wraps around her head, tight enough to thin her hair. She keeps towers of fabric in the sewing room, a city. Her city. You tell him if he ever tries to find her, she will destroy it. From the cotton rubble will come a patterned crane, her crown of gold sequins, her tail of button strings. The sight of it will turn him into drops of freshwater she will drink.

AFRICAN AVIARY

The ibis plucks at dried gumballs blown in at the door. A flock of whistling ducks rounds the pool's edge. The blue-bellied roller forgets its foot is wrapped in netting. The shag paces the painted sand. Orange eyes watch, high in the ebony. The grass owl turns its head to hear the keeper tell the guests whether it is now extinct. A party gathers under the gazebo to play with flamingo chicks. The birthday girl wears a pink puff dress and tells the chicks she is now their mother. The marabous peer into their nest atop the letters. WILD! Their heads knock. The female raises her beak, and rattles from her throat.

NOTES ON TURNING SELF INTO GARDEN
After Ama Codjoe

Compost the colonization of this new world
of Buganda and the ways it made
your grandfathers walk different

This land belonged first
this land once had a different future
Soil can be soaked in rotted paper ballots

until the soil turns red
Our cells absorbed violence until it became us
Maybe centuries is enough

Consume silence
human insulin
a community that calls you *Maama*

You will make mistakes
You will convince yourself that you
can be perfected

You will serve tea to a traitor of the people
Imagine yourself as tall
as Kikaaya Hill

When the ivy you plant begins to creep
you ignore it
lily and lavender

carnations and roses
You water yourself half the recommended amount
until your cheeks begin to yellow

But you survive watching your son
learn to ride a bicycle
You befriend the deer who promise

not to devour in exchange for listening
and the fire ants of the mound
that marks where to turn left to reach you

You refuse to die so the forest
and the queen
grow to respect you

The forest asks for advice
on how to rid itself of vines
The queen reminds you

life came from the ground below your feet
before it was impregnated with foreign seeds
You can grow beauty

for the pleasure of your bloodshot eyes

HAVE YOU BECOME THE DUST?

Before her, death. Grandmother tells the housegirl to clear the doilies from her desk and carry her to sit. She writes to her bazukulu, each a letter. And by the time she reaches the Americans her right hand can just lift a pencil. She writes only questions—big crooked letters with her left. I open the envelope my mother gives me after the funeral. She says there must have been one thousand umbrellas. She says the water soaked her green dress through. Orange clay caked her shoes. She says the smallest children hugged their mothers. The rest danced in the rain.

INK BLOT HELD TO CLOUD

Thanks to the marabou
for breaking
what we cannot.

Acknowledgments

Thank you to the publishers of earlier versions of these poems:
    African American Review: "Marabou", "Found in the African Art Collection…", and "Found in a Connecticut Used Book Store…"
    Afritondo: "Cousins" and "Uncle Writes"
    Obsidian: "Namesake" and "Papaya Tree"
    Torch Magazine: "Notes on Turning Self into Muganda Girl"

Thank you to the team at Small Harbor Publishing for welcoming my writing. Thank you to all who have read drafts of these poems, starting with my classmates and professors in the MFA program at Albertus Magnus College, especially Mad, Michele, and Charles.

Thank you to my community at New Haven Adult & Continuing Education Center. Thank you Obodo Serendipity Books for hosting my first poetry reading. Thank you to my friends for your love and encouragement.

To my family: *Webale nyo* to Maama Senoga for writing *Memoirs Of My Life's Journey* and for your kindness towards me. Thank you to my cousins—I love you all. How are you? Thank you to our grandmother's children: Patrick, Fred, Kate, Sam, Chris, Dorothy, and Baby Rita. Mom, *what's mine is yours.* Thank you Dad for teaching me to find humor in most things. Thank you Grandpa for your love of reading and Grandma Fran for the mailed cards.

Ssuubi, little sister—you told me *go write a poem about it.*

Thank you Michael, Leon, and Soraya. You are my heart.

Glossary

bazukulu: grandchildren

boda: motorcycle taxi

esuuka: wrapper; sleeveless busuuti

Genda webake: Go to sleep.

Gwani?: Who are you?; Who is it?; What is your name?

Gwe olimba: You are lying.

jajja: grandparent

kabalagala: banana pancakes

mwana wange: my child

Otambule mirembe: Travel in peace.

weraba: goodbye; farewell

Rohanna Ssanyu is a black, biracial, and diasporan writer born in Alaska to a mother from Uganda and a father from Missouri. In 2023, her poem "An Aftermath of Empire" won the Nutmeg Poetry Prize organized by the Connecticut Poetry Society, and her poem "Turning Self into Muganda Girl" was nominated for Best of the Net by Torch Literary Arts. She is published in *Obsidian*, *African American Review*, *Literary Mama*, and elsewhere. She holds an MFA from Albertus Magnus College, as well as degrees from Southern Connecticut State University and George Washington University. She lives in Connecticut with her husband and children. She teaches in New Haven. Find Rohanna on Instagram @rohannassanyu.

About Small Harbor Publishing

Small Harbor Publishing is a 501c3 nonprofit organization. Our goal is to publish unique and diverse voices. We are a feminist press, and we are committed to diversity and inclusion. We strive to bring new voices to a devoted and expanding readership.

Small Harbor Publishing began in 2018 with the first issue of *Harbor Review*. The magazine is an online space where poetry and art converse. *Harbor Review* quickly grew and now publishes reviews and runs multiple micro chapbook competitions, including the Washburn Prize and the Editor's Prize.

In July 2020, Small Harbor Publishing was officially incorporated and began Harbor Editions. Harbor Editions accepts submissions through a chapbook open reading period, a hybrid chapbook open reading period, the Marginalia Series, and the Laureate Prize.

In 2023, Harbor Anthologies began with a mission to promote texts that explore social justice issues and highlight marginalized writers.

If you would like to support Small Harbor Publishing, visit our "About" page at: smallharborpublishing.com/about.

www.ingramcontent.com/pod-product-compliance
Lightning Source LLC
Chambersburg PA
CBHW051704040426
42446CB00009B/1293